TWIGS is a Poet!

TWIGS is a Poet!

The Students of
Greenwood Elementary School

iUniverse, Inc.
New York Bloomington

TWIGS is a Poet!

Published by The Greenthumb Publishing Company

iUniverse books may be ordered through booksellers or by contacting:

iUniverse
1663 Liberty Drive
Bloomington, IN 47403
www.iuniverse.com
1-800-Authors (1-800-288-4677)

ISBN: 978-1-4401-6202-2 (pbk)
ISBN: 978-1-4401-6201-5 (ebook)

Printed in the United States of America

iUniverse rev. date: 11/19/09

Table of Contents

Foreword

Greenwood Elementary School is proud to publish the seventh edition of TWIGS, a collection of delightful poems published by our kindergarten through fifth grade students.

Greenwood places a strong instructional focus on writing, including the development of details and voice. TWIGS enables children to understand and apply the writing process and realize that they are accomplished authors.

I would like to acknowledge Greenwood's dedicated teachers who strive for excellence daily and continuous student achievement.

I would also like to recognize our parent support in the collaboration of writing and academic success.

Enjoy the creative collection of poems and join with me in discovering the joy of literacy!

Diane Koenig
Principal
Greenwood Elementary School

Acknowledgements

Once again the staff, students and parent volunteer helpers come together to complete the 7th edition in the TWIGS series. This year's *Twigs is a Poet!* shines throughout with figurative language and creativity fresh from the hearts of children.

Thank you to all those who worked so hard on this year's book. Your dedication allows children to see themselves as authors of both prose and poetry. It is one of the greatest gifts we can give our children!

Dianne L. Bogdan
Editor-in-Chief

Poems of Animals

By Mrs. Miklusak and Mrs. Weber's Classes

Pig
by Anthony Seder

If I had a pig
I would sleep with him.
And then I would run.
Then we would play.
It would be fun to have a pig.

Polar Bears
by Alex Craven

Big strong polar bears
Big white bear that eats seals
A black nosed swimmer

Best Friend
by Sonia Aubrey

Has cool brown eyes
Has a funny cool room
Has hearing aids

All Kinds of Animals
by Sophia Roach

Different funny things
Cute, kind, mean, fun, big, nice, loud
I love animals!!

If I Had a Pig
by Megan Billingsley-Houle

If I had a pig
I would float with him.
And then I would paint.
Then we would fly in a plane.
It would be fun to have a pig.

Sam the Dog
by Thomas Hoffmann

He is nice.
There is the book about Sam.
He loves pizza.
I walk with Sam.

Bear
by Johnathan Larry

He is my friend.
He plays with me.
He watches TV with me.
We go to the movies.

Shadow, My Dog
by Kieran Roehl

Always kisses me
On my face
Barks a lot
Inside and outside
Plays hide and seek
He always finds me.

Free Verse Poems
By Mrs. Brian's Kindergarten

Baths
by Summer DeLong

Baths-
turn on the water
lots of bubbles
splish, splash
water change into waves
turns my fingers into wrinkles
pretending to be a mermaid
soap is a fish swimming.
All clean-
Time for bed!

Parrot
by Tyler Prater

Parrot-
comes in all colors
flies high
cool pet
asks for a cracker.
I want one!

Princesses
by Kylie Perkins

Princesses-
live in a castle
wear beautiful dresses
have glittery crowns
dance at the ball
stay up 'till midnight!

Kitten
by Angel Brown

Here is kitten smiling,
here is kitten sad.
Now you see her sleepy,
now you see her hungry.
Here is kitten in my lap,
sleeping, curled up
taking a nap!

Stars
by Jaden Long

Stars are oh so bright-
Sky you see
only at night!

Colors
by Eric Bean

Colors-
blue,
green,
orange,
purple,
black and brown.
And when I see gray
It makes me frown!

Popcorn
by Meria Seals

I like popcorn-
it's my favorite snack.
Yellow, white,
butter, salt,
Pop! Pop! Pop!

My Bike
by Mary Jay Holton

My bike-
red, white, and blue-
basket with stars-
riding fast-
I wish it was purple!

My Brothers
by Tricia Jackson

My brothers-
older,
bigger
plays with me
ride bikes with me
help me clean my room
Claeton and Bobby are fun!

Motor Scooter
by Nohlan Waters

Motor scooter
fun and fast
put gas in it
ride with my dad-
I want a motor scooter!

Swinging
by Donovan Rey

Swinging-
fun
high
flying
in the sky.

Jared
by Joel Sebastian

My brother-
so funny
makes me laugh
love him!

Chilly the Penguin
by Paul Tyree

Chilly-
Sometimes he's happy,
sometimes he's mad.
Sometimes he is crying,
Sometimes he is glad.
(That is when he is screaming!)

Brothers and Sisters
by Haley Lucas

Sometimes they are mean
sometimes they are nice.
Sometimes they take care of you
when you are sick-
but they are always
made of sugar and spice!

Pizza
by Galate'a Sondey

Pizza, Pizza
I like pizza.
How about you?
Red, sauce
Yellow, cheese
I like pizza.
How about you?

Bike Riding
by Makayla Young

My bike is special
because I like purple.
I ride up the driveway
waving at people.
Riding fast!

Skateboarding
by Justin Webb

Joey skateboards.
He's teaching me how to skateboard too.
He teaches me to Olly.
He teaches me to kick flip.
Skateboarding is fun!

My Bike
by Nakya Thompson

My bike-
really fast
red
go to the park and ride!

Skateboard
by Blake Farrell

Skateboard
rocket speed
jump
flip
go off and on
push and go!

The King
by Ricky Walsh

King-
He's a really nice kid
fought a dragon
saved the princess.
They live in a castle.

Quading
By Anthony Dub

Quading-
off roading fun
in the woods
up high
going fast
spending time with my dad.

School
by Emma Schulz

I like school-
reading
playing Top-It
writing
science
social studies.
Buddies!

Traveling in Space
by Michael Saint Amand

I'm a robot man
going to Jupiter.
I didn't know
where Jupiter was-
so I traveled back
to Earth
and asked my mom!

Family Love Poems

By Mrs. Lamontagne's and Mrs. Baird's First Grade Class

Love
by Tiffani Adkins

Laugh with mom
Outside playing
Very favorite family
Everyday mom hugs me

Love
by Carter Aleck

Laughing together
Outside playing with Cory
Very happy with my mommy
Every day I get kisses from mommy

Love
by Alyssa Armento

Love my family
Out walking with my family
Very happy
Every day I am happy

Love
by Samantha Bailey

Laughing at movie night
Out shopping with mom
Very much fun at the park
Every night kisses

Love
by Jade Boatman

Like watching television with my mom
On rainy days mom and I make crafts
Very happy when we go places together
Every day I go to my cousin's I have fun

Love
by Jalen Chenault

Love my cousins
On the carpet playing
Video games with mom
Each day my mom plays

Love
by Katherine Cohrs

Love playing soccer with my family
On rainy days my family plays hangman
Very happy they are mine
Eat together every night

Love
by Jack Gaches

Love my family
Out playing with my family
Valentine's Day with my family
Eat dinner with family

Love
by Zachary Herendeen

Love my mom
Our outside play days
Very fun playing with my cat
Every day I love my family

Love
by Steven Herman

Love mom and dad
Out to get a Webkinz
Very happy with my family
Every day is fun with them

Love
by Anthony Horak

Laughing
On my bed jumping
Very good dogs
Every day I love my dad

Love
by Antonia Jackson

Like my family
Outside playing with mom
Very happy with dad
Every night I kiss my mom

Love
by Paige Lanphar

Love my mommy
Our family is nice
Very good dad
Every day I am good

Love
by Tyler Miskelly

Love my family
On the carpet playing
Valentine's Day
Every day is fun

Love
by Tristan Mueller

Like my family
Outside
Very happy
Every day I play with my brother

Love
by Ashley Phillips

Laying together to read
Our family is great
Very good family
Every day I get kisses

Love
by Celeste Silva

Love mom and dad
Oh good family
Very nice dad
Every day I hug my mom

Love
by Shane Simovski

Like going to my papa's
Oh I love my family
Very good dinners from dad
Enjoy reading with mom

Love
by Jacob Webb

Laughing with Nicholas
On the trampoline
Valentine hugs from mom
Every time I get a kiss

Love
by Qwynn Willert

Love mom
Outside playing with my brothers
Very nice mom
Easy to love mom

Spring Poems

By Mrs. Clancy's First Grade

Easter
by Jimmy Scheid

I enjoy Easter.
I like it, I get presents.
Easter is so fun!

Easter
by Evan Dawson

Easter eggs are good.
Easter bunnies jump around.
Spring is when he comes!

Rabbits
by Ashlenn Waters

Rabbits like to bounce.
They leave us a lot of toys.
They are really cute.

Bunnies
by Jenna Kochanski

I love brown bunnies,
Because they are cute and small.
Bunnies come in Spring!

Rabbits
by Khalil Ford

Rabbits are so cute.
They are spotted and furry.
They feel very soft.

Flowers
by Gracie Allor

Flowers are pretty.
Petals are soft and pretty.
I love flowers!

Easter
by Corra Lucas

The Easter bunny,
Is busy passing out eggs.
Happy Easter Day!

Easter
by Taylor Kleist

On Easter morning,
Found a brown bunny.
The bunny was soft.

Bunnies
by Kelsie Simons

A pink mom bunny,
Has babies in the spring.
They are so cute!

Rabbits
by Ifiyenia Zisopoulos

Rabbits are pretty.
Rabbits love to eat grass.
Rabbits are cute too!

Easter Bunny
by Abby Cipponeri

The Easter bunny
He brings eggs everyday.
I love the bunny!

Spring Flowers
by Chrissy Layer

Violets are beautiful,
When they bloom. They smell pretty.
They are so cool!

Flowers
by Grace Wojciechowski

Watch the flowers grow!
Look at the flowers growing!
They are beautiful!

Spring Flowers
by Jacob Caruso

A spring flower blooms.
Petals are soft and pretty.
They smell beautiful!

Easter
by Dominic Hill

I like Easter day!
The bunny hides my basket.
I have to find it!

Bunnies
by Taylor Ferry

Bunnies are so cute.
Bunnies like to play a lot.
Bunnies like to jump!

Bunnies
by Kenny Buchanan

Bunnies are so cute.
The bunnies like to jump high.
That's why I like them.

Rabbits
by Edward Bailey

A little rabbit
The rabbit was jumping high.
I really like him!

Easter
by Jason Daniel

On Easter morning,
Look for my Easter basket.
Easter is so fun!

Easter
by Kelly May

I love Easter day!
The Easter bunny brings eggs.
I love the bunny!

All about Us

By Mrs. Rustoni's Second Grade Class

All About Me
by Cassidy Holton

Caring
Artist
Silly
So cool
Interesting
December
Yo-Yo lover

All About Me
by Emily Duncan

Excited
My favorite color is purple
I like ice cream
Loving
Young

All About Me
by Jared Bialecki

Joyful
Apple eater
Runner
Enjoys skate boarding
Dare devil

All About Me
by Kylie Gore

Kind
Yakker
Laugher
Ice cream maker
Eats carrots

All About Me
by Alayna Clancy

Artist
Learner
Acrobat
Yo-Yo trick learner
Net catcher
Apple lover

All About Me
by Nate Bober

Nice
Age seven
Thomas The Train collector
Eats pizza

All About Me
by Gjuljeta Biblekaj

Good at soccer
Joyful
Understanding
Love my family
Joker
Expert at science
Trustworthy
Artist

All About Me
by Katie Hurley

Kind
Alive
Terrific
I'm cute
Explainer

All About Me
by Samantha Bursteinowicz

Special
Adorable
Marvelous
A really good singer
Nice
Terrific
Harmless
Angelic

All About Me
by Jessica Woods

Joyful
Elephant liker
Science lover
Silly
Is cute
Calls her friends
Artist

All About Me
by Katie Turner

Kind
Artist
Trustworthy
I like my family
Entertaining

All About Me
by Morgan Sawchuk

Magnificent
Over The Hedge lover
Rain player
Great
Animal lover
Nice

All About Me
by Seanna Saccone

Sensitive
Expert at soccer
Attractive
Nice
Neat
Athlete

All About Me
by Marissa Prantera

More than nice
Artist
Respectful
Incredible
Sassy
Silly
Adorable

All About Me
by David Peddicord

Double dipper
Artist
Very good at math
Ice cream eater
Detroit Tiger fan

All About Me
by Nathan Myers

Nice
Active
Talkative
Hungry
Alive
Nutty

All About Me
by Emily Litz

Egg eater
Magician
Ice cream maker
Laughs a lot
Yard player

All About Me
by Andrea Lanham

Artist
Nice
Destined to be a singer
Reliable
Expert
Active

All About Me
by Madison Klimowicz

Matter to my family
Apple eater
Dog lover
Dynamite
Important
Expert at science

All About Me
by Samantha Kemp

Smart
Alive
Musical
Artist
Nice
Trustworthy
Healthy
Attractive

All About Me
by Claeton Jackson

Chatty
Like Penguins
Always working
Energy
Tall
Outstanding
Nice

All About Me
by Michael Agresta

Michael's cool
Impossible to beat in math games
Cake eater
Hates getting behind
A video game nerd
Eli Manning fan
Likes football

Thoughts Expressed in Haiku
By Mrs. Balmas' Third Grade

My Mom
by Catlyn Bizzotto

My mom is my day.
I love my mother so much.
She is the best mom.

Mrs. Balmas
by Zachary Allor

She is my teacher.
She is always really nice.
I like her a bunch.

My Dog and I
by Samuel Waskowksi

We have to play now.
I love to play fetch with her.
I love my puppy.

The Good Look
by Madison Gollehur

She gives me a look,
I could see that very smile.
She makes me happy.

Mom
by Vincent Layer

My mom is my life.
My mom always stands by me.
My mom is my day.

Austin
by Gage Sheridan

He stands up for me,
He is the best friend ever.
He is a true friend.

My Dog
by Jordan Sebastian

My dog pulled my hair.
I do not know what to do!
No treat for her now.

My Pet Penny
by Brandon Crump

My dog is hyper!
She is also silly, too.
She is a good dog.

Clarissa
by Katlyn Zerillo

She is shy but fun.
She is the sun in summer.
She's a rainbow, too.

My Friend Sammy
by Brad Tyree

He is cool and strange,
He is a very nice friend.
I like him so much.

My Dog Sunny
by Leilani Eib

He's very restless-
Never not under my feet,
But I still love him.

Belle
by Samantha Smith

Belle listens to me.
My dog Belle is nice and good.
She catches snowballs.

Fish
by Blake Bastian

Fish swim in water.
Fish swim majestically,
Such scaly wet fish!

Katlyn
by Meranda Boland

My best friend is fun.
She's a sun and she plays nice.
I like her a lot.

Tiger
by Clarissa Leggieri

My cat is fluffy.
He runs outside all day long.
He's my only cat.

My Mom, Heather
by Jae'A Mellon

She is really nice.
She's like a rainbow to me.
She is the best mom.

My Cat Patch
by Lauren Lilly

I have a fat cat.
She's very cute and fuzzy.
I love her so much.

TV
by Corey Aleck

It is fun to watch.
It also has lots of shows.
I watch it a lot.

Snow!!

By Mrs. Flaherty's Third Grade Class

Snow
by Ian Bass

Santa is coming.
Nobody is awake.
On the day Santa gives presents we'll be happy
We will love Christmas!

Winter
by Erin May

Wonderful snowflakes fall.
Icicles on every house.
Nice people go caroling.
The wind blows hard.
Everyone is inside.
Reindeer fly at night.

Winter
by Nicholas Webb

Winter is here.
In the winter snowflakes fall.
Never to late to put on hats and gloves.
To learn how to like winter you must learn to like snow.
Ever make a snowball?
Right next to my house there is a huge snow pile!

Snow
by Jordan Harris

Snow is awesome! Especially the snowball fights.
No snow is no fun.
On Christmas it's really fun! (Because you can have snowball fights)
Without Christmas it would be terrible.

Snow
by Melody Momper

Snow is falling.
Nuts or chestnuts cracking.
Out of the chimney comes Santa Claus.
Winter is almost gone except for the holiday spirit.

Snow
by Hannah Ver

Scarves and mittens kee
Naughty kids do not ge
Ornaments are hanging
Winter is here!

Wl
It i
Nc
Th
Ev
Rc

Winter
by Gjozofina Bib

We go on a snowmobile
In the snow we have a sn
There are snowmen comir
Everybody run!
Reindeer go on a sleigh wi

Snow
by Madison DeSa

Snow is on the ground.
Now all of the icicles are hanging
On Christmas Santa comes.
We all play in the snow.

Wor
Iglc
Nev
The
Ever
Rud

Snow
by Anna Pellerit

Snow flakes fall dowr
Now we open our pr
Our mom gives us pre
Wow, I see Santa!

Winter
by Devin Young

at wonderful snow flakes are dropping!
winter time here.
w let's play.
 snow is here .
ryone is playing.
ing around in the snowball war, they had fun.

Snow
by Madison Rakus

Snow is beautiful!
Night is beautiful!
Outside it is snowing!
Winter is fun!

Winter
by Catherine Bucholtz

derful snowflakes falling to the ground.
s are made by little kids.
r get frostbite, it will hurt.
ir is getting cold. It is time to wear hats and mittens.
 kid is playing outside.
lph's nose lights up like a flashlight.

Winter
by Brandon Cerulli

Wonderful! It is a snow day.
I want a gingerbread man.
Naughty kids get coal.
The snow is cold.
Every kid should get a gift.
Rare gifts are saved for good kids.

Snow
by Stevie Smith

Sometimes in snow it's cold.
Now we all open presents.
On Christmas a lot of penguins are happy because of snow.
We all get awesome presents.

Snow
by Brendan Fick

Snowflakes are falling on the ground.
No don't eat the snow-- it's too cold.
Ornaments are hanging on the tree.
Wow there's an igloo with a penguin in it in the North Pole.

Snow
by Austin Whitmore

Snowmen are fun to make.
No one believes in Santa Claus.
On Christmas I got presents.
Winter is cool!

Snow
by Brooke Patroske

Santa's coming down the chimney.
No presents under the tree yet.
Open the presents in the morning.
Winter is so fun.

Winter
by Christopher Silva

Wow it is snowing!
Inside my house I have a tree.
Nutcrackers are cracking nuts.
The tree is shining bright.
Enjoying my food.
Running and jumping into snow.

Winter
by Eleni Zisopoulos

Winter is a wonderful season.
Igloos might be uncomfortable to sleep in.
Naughty kids do not get presents.
The snow is freezing.
Everybody is in bed when Santa comes.
Rudolph is the head reindeer.

Snow
by Victoria Cipponeri

Snow balls are fun to throw.
No more cookies says Mom.
On Christmas we say, "Yeah!"
Winter is here.

Silly Limerick Poems

By Mrs. Heiss and Mrs. Sullivan's Fourth Grade Class

Stick and Brick
by Alicia Papuga

I once knew a very high stick
Would you believe his first name was Rick?
He always sat down
And often had a frown
He had a friend named Brick

A Goo-Eating Bear
by Peter Chen

Once my hair had a blue doo
It turned to a giant glob of glue
A bear ate my hair
And I ate the bear
Then my hair started growing goo

Pool Wars
by Cody Colbert

I once had a really big pool
It was so very cool
A monster was in there
He had bright red hair
And then we had a duel

The Bee
by Jessie Memetaj

I once had a small pet bee
Of course it had stung me
I was surprised
That he apologized
So then I named him Lee

My Pet Bear
by Maria Fantuzzi

I once had a pet bear
It wore my underwear
It slept in my bed
And my face turned red
So I just sat in my chair

The Tar Bar
by James Schell

I once had a glob of gooey tar
Off I went to the smoky bar
I drank some root beer
I shed a little tear
Then away I went in my tiny car

The Dead Bee
by John Klimowicz

I once knew a very weird bee
And his name was "Knee"
He lived in a shoe
Right next to Lou
And sadly he died as sea

The Blue Phone
by Katie Chess

I once had a very blue phone
That turned into a cone
I started to eat
But it turned into a beet
And then turned into a bone

A Man Named Corey
By Corey Groves

There once was a man named Corey
His nickname was Lori
He was very shy
He's lucky he didn't die
Thank God it was a story

A Bear Named Tom
by Jacob Richard

Once I had a bear named "Tom"
He threw a large paint bomb
It hit a house
Out ran a mouse
And along came Tom's mom

The Big Black Bear
by Paul Willard

I once had a big black bear
That had very curly hair
Then his hair turned soft
Which made him live in a loft
Then this bear, he became a hare

The Small Shoe
by Michael Capaldi

Once I had a very small shoe
Do you believe it played the kazoo?
I bought it at a store
And the dollars were four
I believe it was named Lou

The Fat Cat
by Mikayla Pomeroy

I once had a big black cat
Who liked to sit on a mat
This cat loved tuna
And he was a puma
After that this cat grew fat

My Rabbit
by Rachel Malaga

My rabbit loves to act like she died
She goes away so she can hide
She can hop all around
Bother me till I drown
She likes her food to be fried

Scary Larry and Harry
by Justin Powers

There once was a man named Larry
Who had a friend named Harry
They liked to dance about
Day in and day out
And often it was scary

Hey, Look, a Bear
by Dylan Armstrong

When I was eating a pear
I spotted a big brown bear
He ate lots of salami
He loved bear origami
And I saw him grow some hair

Moo
by Hilary Cosley

I once had a dog named Moo
He loved to eat tofu
He'd eat all day
And then he'd say
"Oh how I love kung fu!"

Joe Shmoe
by Chris Holstine

Not so very long ago,
There was a guy named Joe Shmoe
He lived to play ball
Down a long hall
And he made a lot of dough

Kalamazoo
by Danny Litz

I once went to the zoo
I saw a very big shoe
It had a huge door
With a very small core
After, I left for Kalamazoo

A Baby Named Joe
by Zack Gerniski

Not so long ago
There came along Bobby Joe
He liked to run
And just get things done
He just liked to go with the flow

Larry the Berry
by Andrew Herman

There once was a man named Larry the Berry
And Larry was very hairy
From his head to his toes
And even on his red nose
He met Mary who was also hairy

Fun Poems

By Mrs. Dzubak's Fourth Grade Class

Autobiographical Poem
by Cory Kupinski

Cory
Dude, smart, cool
Brother of Austin
Who loves tacos, salsa and beef
Who feels good about soccer
Who gives jokes, tips and cheats
Who fears spiders
Who would like to see Alaska
Who dreams of joining M.L.S.
A student of Mrs. Dzubak
Cory

Makes Me Think Of
by Jordan Knudsen

Summer makes me think of football
Football makes me think of mud
Mud makes me think of showering
Showering makes me think of rain
Rain makes me think of summer

Autobiographical Poem
by Larry Plotnisky

Larry
Crazy, nice, kind
Brother to Jason and Shannon
I love basketball, baseball, and cheese bread
Who feels nice and kind
Who needs more baseball, Playstation 3, Xbox 360
I fear hurt, pain and stitches

Silly Poem
by Camden Kosal

Adam ate a cookie while Bobby ate a cake
Camden had a pie
Donna drank a shake
Erika drank water
Freddy stole an apple
Grandpa had a cheesecake and won't be back for a while

The Yack
by Zack Shadowens

There's this thing called a Yack.
It lives on your back
He bites and bites until you go wack and
If you try to smash him you will not find him
Because he is as small as a flea and
If you miss him he will go pee.
So try not to get one of these fantastic things,
You'll only find him in the Sahara Desert.

Fishy
by A.J. Stonik

One day I went fishing, I even caught a girl fishy.
She howled and scowled, she flipped and she flopped
She looked like she was about to pop.
But I put her in the water, then I saw her drop.

Apples
by Janae Daniel

Apples are really, really good!
Bad apples are very nasty.
Cold apples are freezing on my teeth
Don't eat hot apples, they get mushy inside
Eat rotten apples and you will feel yucky
Fruity apples are delicious
Go out and pick red and green apples
How big do apples grow?
I don't like sour apples
Janae loves sweet apples

Skateboard
by Joshua Frost

Start skating today
Keep trying until you get it
All day fun
Time your Ollie
Every day, all day, forever
Bails hurt bad at times
Ollie high if possible
Always have fun
Ride jumps and find skate spots
Decide if you want to go pro

Makes Me Think Of
by Celeste Bingle

Surfboarding makes me think of waves
Waves make me think of water.
Water makes me think of rain.
Rain makes me think of sadness.
Sadness makes me think of people.
People make me think of surfboarding.

Mom
by Adam Bean

Sweet, kind
She is active
She is in my heart
Amazing

The Note to Santa
by Erika Smith

I gave him my milk and my cookies and all I got was this
brush.
Every single Christmas, I always give him a note saying, "I
want more stuff!"
The only thing I get is stupid little things.
It has to end!
I'm really mad.
Why don't I get as much as other kids?
I'm going into fourth grade.
I need presents now!
Signed,
Mad at you!

Autobiographical Poem
by Kelsie Gore

Beautiful, kind and fun
Sister of Kylie
Who loves Romeo, Jeff and friends
Who feels excited about High School Musical 3
Who needs friends, attention and love
Who gives money, food and friendship
Who fears the dark and Kylie
Who would like to meet Vanessa Hudges
Who dreams of being an actress
A student of Mrs. Dzubak
Kels

Makes Me Think Of
by Kortney Hepting

Friends make me think of Kelsie
Kelsie makes me think of flowers
Flowers make me think of Ally
Ally makes me think of shopping
Shopping makes me think of Erika
Erika makes me think or friends!

Autobiographical Poem
by Marty Gulewicz

Builder, folder, funny
Brother of Drew
Who loves Dad, Mom, and Ryan
Who feels happy about war
Who needs an Xbox 360, PS3, and a Game Cube
Who gives Wii, DS, and Xbox
Who would like to see George Washington
Who dreams of being rich
A student of Mrs. Dzubak
Marty

Oranges
by Erin Kaveloski

I was writing about my lovely love for oranges, but then I
came to a problem. I couldn't find a word to rhyme with
oranges. I came to this:
"I love my lovely oranges so beautiful and divine and it even
rhymes with..."
I was stuck. Orange, porange, no
Orange, loranges, no, No, NO!
I think I'll write about apples.

Exaggerating Sister
by Allyson Humphrey

I have a little sister who thinks jelly beans can dance.
She said she dropped a jelly bean and the jell bean was mean
And he started to dance.
She said he went flop, pop, and started to mop.
Or as I can say, my sister has a big imagination.

Autobiographical Poem
by Victor Radecki

Victor
Funny, smart, active
Brother of Connie, Corine and Cala
Who loves games, magazines and Game Stop
Who feels good about games
Who needs food, friends and family
Who gives money, pencils, and things
Who fears bad grades, losing rights and not having video games
Who would like to see no war
Who dreams of being rich
A student of Mrs. Dzubak
Vic

Loving
by Christina Mominee

Lots of love
Obviously very sweet
Very fun
In the air
Never stops loving
Giving love

Dave
by Michael Turner

Dad like no other
A nice dad
Very nice to all
Eats a lot

Michael
by Michael LaBarbera

Michael
Funny, cool, wanting
Brother of Robby and son of Sue and Tony
Who loves books, playing and gym
Who feels good about reading
Who needs entertainment, lots of food, shelter
Who fears spiders, heights, and falling off things
Who would like to see his grandma
Who dreams of being an artist
A student of Mrs. Dzubak

Cats
by Kaitlyn McCain

Cats
Cute, sweet
Sleepy, cuddly, kid
Nice, fun, funny love
Small

Opposite Poem
by William DeSchutter

Girl
Pretty, loving
Shopping, talking, laughing
Giggling, actress, skateboarder, actor
Gamer, surfing, fixing cars
Handsome, strong
Boy

Giggle Poem
by Robert Jackson

I heard a kid
Who burped in school
Everybody was silent
And there it went again
If he doesn't stop
This whole class is gonna drop!

My Friend
by Jarrett Caruso

Josh
Funny, talented
He is an athlete
He is my best friend
Mad, sad, happy, great
Joshua

Winter is a Wonderful Season!

By Mrs. Bogdan's Fifth Grade Class

The Best Christmas
by Tony Fantuzzi

Cold as ice in the freezer
Like you don't even know
Beep! Beep!
Hot cocoa is ready
Presents below the tree
Until I go outside
I'll be warming my feet
All over town
Up in the sky
Snowflakes falling from high
Behind all Christmas
This is the best!

Winter
by Suzanne Sweetwood

Icicles hanging from the houses
Snowflakes falling on the grass
Snowballs flinging in the air
Children running everywhere
Presents under the tree
The lights all over town
Carolers singing on the front porch
Fires burning in the fireplace
Ice skating in the rink
A snowman by the park
Waiting to be built
The star on the tree
Will make it complete
As white as a wedding dress
I like winter the best!

Winter Fun
by Jackie Krolczyk

Into winter
Snowy winds
Out the door
Happy grins
To the snow hill
With our sleds
Skating in a cold rink
Getting something hot to drink
Winter is fun!

Winter Fun
by Yasmina Maksimovski

Snowball fights
Playing in the snow
With friends
Hot chocolate
To the warm the insides
Sleepovers in winter
Making big snow angels
Staying indoors
Watching movies
Trips to Frankenmuth
For holiday fun
I don't like winter
But I can still have fun!

Winter
by Jasmine Livings

Time for ice skating
Time for hot chocolate
In December
In January
Fires for warmth
Santa for gifts
Hills for sledding
Christmas tree for Christmas
Ornaments for the tree
Lights for the tree
Time for Christmas!

Winter Fantasy
by Cameron Fick

Around the corner
A blizzard is coming
Hot chocolate for the microwave
Ready to drink
Near the snow fort
A snowball attacks!
Instead of summer
Winter is here!
Since there's no snowballs in summer
Use your time wisely in winter!

Winter
by Hannah Bialecki

As cold as a popsicle
As white as frosting
Around the corner
Snowballs are thrown
A new snowman built in snow
Snowflakes all around the town
Penguins waddling all around
Hot cocoa in the microwave
Presents under the tree
The fire is up and toasty
Stars are shining brightly!

Winter
by Maddy Glendenning

Snow is falling above and below us
Beyond me are carolers singing
Beneath me is snow up to my knees
Wishing upon stars hoping Santa Claus is coming
Down the streets there is nothing but shining lights
As if they have been working for years!
With lights shining among the snow
Outside I see no leaves or birds
Hot chocolate burning my throat
Presents under the tree!

Winter Fantasy
by Ally Powell

Around the corner
Like a blizzard of sprinkles
In comes winter
Along the street
Snowballs fly
Like little birds in the sky
Joy is flowing through the house
Christmas ornaments on the tree
Shining like little diamonds.
The smell of cookies in the kitchen
Grandma's house warm and cozy
Winter is the best season ever!!

Winter
by Matthew Hinze

Near Christmas
As white as ice cream
Outside throwing snowballs
Inside drinking hot chocolate
By a fire in your house
Christmas tree set up inside
Setting up designs outside
Skiing with my friends at Christmas break!

Winter
by James May

Around the house I look
Up until I find the cold sensation
Beneath the gutter of my house
Onto the roof
I go to get an icicle
Christmas is around the corner
On the side of the chimney
Santa fell to the ground
Beyond the clouds Santa flies
So I say good night!

Snowballs
by Adam Akers

Snowballs thrown
Around a corner
Snow getting picked up
Formed into a ball
Snow going down
Your back
Icy cold
Snow forts sitting
On the ground
Getting plowed like a giant snowball
Hitting you
Building snow walls
Shoveling
Snow getting packed
Going up and down!

Winter Fantasy
by Marina Saccone

Around the corner
Like sprinkles poured on cookies
Christmas waits
Ornaments dangling
On the tree
Hot chocolate sits beside me
Snow free falling from the sky
As far as my eye can see
Christmas time is near!

Winter Fun!
by Maria Mlynarek

Christmas time is here
Ho! Ho! Ho!
Cold as ice
Snowy blizzard out in the cold
Hot chocolate at night
Gingerbread cookies
Presents in the morning
Snowboarding in the snow
Slipping and sliding
A shining star in the sky
A Christmas tree bright as the sun
Snowmen dancing around
Ornaments dangling from the tree

Winter Fantasy
by Mario Oldani

Cold as ice
Dangling icicles
Ornaments as sparkly as the sun
Snowflakes whirling like the wind
Christmas time is near
Hot chocolate in the microwave
Snow beyond the eye can see
Joy throughout the world
Down the chimney is Santa Claus
Christmas is near
As white as snow
Like a slurpee
Between December and January
Underneath a blanket of snow.
Despite the cold from each house
Throughout the world there is peace

Christmas
by Colton Bodnar

Around the corner
In comes Christmas
In the living room
On with the glow
Of the tree
Until the cat unplugs the lights
With me bouncing about
I wake my parents
Presents underneath the tree
I rip my first
Within the gift
A new game system for me
That would be
Like the best Christmas ever!

Winter
by Samantha Leonardi

As cold as a popsicle
White as frosting
Ice as long as a child
Vacation as cold as ever
Under 10 degrees Fahrenheit
Christmas is near
Let out a big cheer
Presents and trees are here and near!
Hot chocolate, cider, playing in the snow
What are you waiting for?
Let's go, go, go!

The Winter Feeling
by Mallory Price

Across the skyline
Like a dream
Into the sky
Where the sun shines
On the snow
As I walk the white
Like a freezer outside
Underneath all the snow
Is still the green remember
It will be spring
As fast as light
I wish it would never end!

Winter
by Marshall Moise

Around the corner
Watch out!
Snowballs flying toward me
As cold as a popsicle
It's white as Frosty the Snowman
A blizzard is around the corner
Cause it is about to be
Winter! Winter!
I spend it always with my family
Parents buying presents for everyone
Winter is over!

Winter
by Evan Cybak-Vertin

Family means the most to me
House filled with joy
Grandma cooks
Mom helping
Dad watching football
Brandon too
Playing a new game
What a blast is Christmas Day!

Winter
by Gregory Silva

White as Santa's beard
Cold as ice
Around the corner
Outside the cold weather
I'm with my family
I'm inside my house
Under the Christmas tree
I see presents
I'm going out to see
The Lion King movie!

Winter Fun!
by Haley McCain

Winter is around the corner
Sitting on the ground
Playing in the snow
There's icicles hanging
From the house like a dangling chandelier
Ornaments on a Christmas tree shining like crystal
On the house are bright Christmas lights
As bright as a star shining in the night
Candy canes as yummy as snow
I can't wait until the presents come this way!
Mmmmm! Hot chocolate as hot as a stove!

Winter Fun
by Trevor Rakus

Family means the most to me
Because they love me
Snowboarding on a slanted mountain
Watching the Christmas story
Seeing my brother
See Alvin and the Chipmunks!

Snow
by Ivan Aubrey

Like little falling stars
As white as the new fallen snow
Snowflakes are finally here!
Snow is its falling friend in the air
Around, around
Wind blows all around
Snowflakes, snow, and wind
Are winter's best friends!

Winter
by Corina Cunningham

No school for vacation
Friends come over
Presents under the Christmas tree
Family together
Snow on the ground
Throwing snowballs
Making snowmen
Dogs playing in the snow
Winter is awesome!

Winter Poetry Fun!
By Mrs. Thomas' Fifth Grade Class

Snowball Fights
by David Turner

Snowballs, snowballs, snowball Fights
Snowball wars with family and friends
Fun, cold, thrilling, chilling
Snowballs, snowballs, snowball fights!
Try not to get hit
Try not to get nailed
Snow balls, snow balls, snow ball fights
Make a fort, make some snow balls like soft white rocks
Snow balls, snow balls, snow balls fights!

A Snow Day
by Gaige Wegner

The snow is falling
The trees are shaking
The children are shivering
A snowman like a snow covered tree
When all the children play
Spread Christmas cheer
For all to hear
On Maple Street I see a Christmas tree
All bright and full of light
Another snow day it may be!

My Beautiful Snowman
by Molly Krist

Snowman, oh snowman
You shimmer like new snow
You have a bright carrot nose
As spring is coming
You melt down like an ice cube
I'll miss you snowman
I hope to see you
The next winter to come

Snowflakes
by Alexis Vallee

Snowflakes are falling
Sparkle, glimmer
Snowflakes are falling
Quicker and quicker
Looks like spices
Falling low
Comes with us
Where ever we go!

Winter Snow
by Kayla Oakey

Winter snow
As white as a cloud
Winter snow
We should be proud
The trees are rustling
The wind is blowing
All so calm and clear
The taste of hot cocoa
Warms my body
Please snow
Don't go away!

Snow
by Sabrina Justin

As the snow falls,
Its giant snowballs
I hear shivering children
Day and night
It sounds like bells jingling
In the snow
I hear families having fun
Until the day is done!

A Winter Fantasy
by Neal Backus

Snowflakes are falling
All over town
Slipping, sliding
Everybody rushing around
There's an icy chill in the air
Telling us that winter
Is really here
Frost on the window
Snow on the ground
Looks like mashed potatoes
All over town!

Snow
by Jordan Eckman

Sparkly, sparkly snow
Oh, I wish you never have to go
You glimmer and glimmer
In the moonlight
To all you go near
You bring joy to people
You bring families together
With holiday cheer!

Snowflakes
by Ashley Martyniuk

White snowflakes
Falling down
With sparkly friends
The give me the shivers
All the quivers
Snowflakes falling
Falling low
Looks like sprinkles
Falling down!

Snow
by Sage Williard

Snow is like a star shining
Shining in the sky
Snow is like a piece of paper
Clean and white
Snow is like a delight
Fun and white
Snow is like a kitty
Playing in the snow
Snow is like a sparkle
In the light!

Snowflakes
by Jennifer Eckenwiler

Snowflakes falling on my head
It's very beautiful
My mom said
It glimmers and it glitters
It gives me the shivers
As smooth as a white fluffy white blanket
It makes no sound
On the ground
The sun came out I see
I do not want the snow to leave
It is leaving
There is no doubt
I will have a very
Big pout!

Snowflakes
by Matt Hall

Snowflakes look like
Cotton balls
Falling from the sky
Kids making snowmen
Running everywhere
Snowboarding, sledding
On the hill
Friends throwing snowballs
Time to go home now
Let's go to bed
Merry Christmas to all
And all a good night!

Snowman
by David Silva

Snowman, snowman as cold as you can be
Come and play with me
Slipping, slipping on the snow
Come on! Let's go
It's getting late
I must go to bed
Wait it is nice and cozy
No one is noisy
Good morning, good morning snowman
Let's get up and play
There is no time to wait
For the next day
It's shiny and hot as hot as can be
Snowman is out go and see Santa

Winter
by Austin Stabile

One storm on a beautiful day
I let my dog out to go and play
Then I went to let her in
She was covered with snow
She looked like a white alien
That was the funniest thing
I've ever seen!

First Snow
by Josh Canter

When the first snowball is made
It is just like an army
Battle has begun
The first thing to do is to fire back
When a snowball is not so good
It blows in your face
And you see the glow!

Snow Day
by Jacob Combs

Snowfalls on the lawn
Hearing kids cheer with glee
Going Christmas shopping
Snowball fights
Hot chocolate I smell
Oh how nice!
Waking up one morning
Looking out the window
Seeing snow
It looks like a giant fluffy blanket!

Snowman
by Hannah Bulick

I go outside to have some fun
Then I see some people run
I wonder why they are running
Then I look down the street
And I see a snowman coming!
A snowman comes up to me
Oh, someone help, oh please, oh please
I'll say it on my knees
Bye! Bye! Snowman
I hope you had fun
But now it's time for us to run!

Snow Day
by Maddie Schulz

Snowflakes as light as feathers
Fell on our snow day
Bright lights and snowball fights
On our cold snow day
Snowmen sit upon the ground
Without making a single sound
All these wonders will await
On a snow day that's really great!

Snowman
by Unknown Author

Eyes of coal
Orange carrot nose
Hat with read ribbon around it
White fluffy body of snow
Brown twig arms
Bye! Bye! Snowman
I hope you had fun
But now it's time for us to run!

Snow Falls
by Kobe Willert

Snow falls all day an night
It comes and goes
It shines when the moon lights
It looks like crystals
Shining on you
Oh, no! The sun's back
Bye! See you next year!

Snow
by Shelby McCombs

Snow goes
Snow stays
Falls down
Like trees
Shaking in the breeze
Snow at knees
Snowmen, Snowwomen
Snowball, snow fights
All the fun
We'll have tonight!

Snow
by Jeremiah Hardy

Snow as high as mountains
Snowflakes falling
The winds are calling
Right through your ears
As you deck the halls
Someone starts to call
Your name in a voice you can't hear
Now all you have to do
Is make sure you have a great holiday cheer!

Snow
by Jacob Allor

One day when I awoke
And saw the snow
It was like a million Arctic hares
Standing next to each other
When I looked at the front lawns
Snowmen and igloos were made
Just until a snowstorm came
And swept the snowmen and igloos away!

Snow Day
by Ian Phillips

It's a snow day so fluffed and white
Oh, how I just can't wait
Until I jump in to you
But I am grounded
So all the kids but me
Can play in the snow
So have fun In the snow
While I lay in my bed
As you play in the snow
I will stare at the ceiling
What you say it is Wednesday?
I am so happy
I am not grounded!
Good-bye room!
See you next June!